Spelling
Made Easy

by VIOLET BRAND

LEVEL ONE
SAM AND THE TRAMP

EGON PUBLISHERS LTD
Royston Road, Baldock, Hertfordshire SG7 6NW

First impression 1984
Second impression 1985
Third impression 1986
Fourth impression 1988
Fifth impression 1988
Sixth impression 1989
Seventh impression 1989
Eighth impression 1990
Ninth impression 1991
Tenth impression 1991
by Egon Publishers Ltd.
Royston Road, Baldock, Herts SG7 6NW

Copyright © Egon Publishers Ltd.
and Violet Brand

ISBN 0 905858 25 5

Printed in England by
Streetsprinters
Royston Road, Baldock,
Herts SG7 6NW

Level 1

The multi-sensory methods of teaching spelling seem to have been over-looked in the main-stream of education since World War II. Too much emphasis has been placed on learning to spell through visual methods. The ears and the mouth have been forgotten and the power of the hand ignored.

If a child, or an adult, hears a sequence of sounds, sees them visually represented, feels the sequence in his mouth and reproduces the symbols with his hand, his awareness of the basis of written language is awakened. He feels that he can control it — and what he controls he can use. No one sense is left to flounder and the fear of the printed word which so often besets adult illiterates and failing teenagers is removed. The senses which they employ for normal communication, speech and hearing, are being involved in the written language which has previously defeated them.

If a young child is encouraged to listen and say, as well as to look, the multi-sensory approach to literacy skills can begin before motor skills are far enough advanced for the child to actually write. Once primary education has begun, multi-sensory methods can be used to prevent future failure.

Experience of teaching spelling through a wide age range, from 6 year olds to adults and through a wide ability range, from slow learners to University students, has convinced me that the English language needs to be presented in a structured way, so that a knowledge of its regular phonic pattern is easily acquired. Word family groupings should therefore form the basis of the teaching of spelling.

The teaching order of word families should take into consideration:

(a) the number of common words, over which the child, or adult, needs to acquire control early in his literacy life.

(b) the establishment of certain common principles that affect the sound of letters

   (i)   The doubling of a vowel (ee)

   (ii) the combination of a vowel and a consonant (ar)

   (iii) the combination of two consonants (sh)

   (iv) the effect of a silent 'e' on a vowel (cake)

(v) the combination of two vowels (ai)

(vi) the grouping of two or more letters to produce one sound (igh, air)

and

(c) the desirability of keeping trouble apart, i.e. separating ir, ur, er, by a few weeks.

It is suggested that whilst the teaching of word families should start with the basic vowel sounds, these should not be taught in alphabetical order. A child, or adult, with spelling problems often has great difficulty in hearing the difference between the basic sound of ă * and the basic sound of ĕ. It is therefore better to follow teaching of ă words, with teaching of ŏ words. It you have doubts, open your mouth and say aloud ă. Then say ĕ. Listen to your voice and feel what happens to the shape of your mouth. Very little you may think. Repeat the exercise with ă and ŏ and then with ŏ and ĭ.

ᵕIndicates short vowel sound.

Only one word family should be taught a week, irrespective of the age of the student. The point at which the teaching starts will vary with the age and stage the student has reached.

Many 6-8 year olds can benefit by work on the basic vowel sounds, whilst becoming accustomed to multi-sensory teaching methods. Illiterate teenagers and adults desperately need work on basic vowel sounds and cannot make progress without. Almost all 7-8 year olds would find spelling much easier if they were taught one digraph* a week and the jump from basic vowel sounds to digraphs is often the sticking point for older children and adults.

* two or more letters making one sound.

Basic words that are needed before they have been reached phonically, or that have no phonic base, represent another element in the teaching of spelling. Finger tracing, and the more advanced stages of this method, as used by Grace Fernald, should be employed.

At any age, the spelling stage reached by the child/student, should be checked. Therefore, at each level, test dictations, are included to assist the teacher.

4

If gaps in knowledge, poor sequencing skills and the constant re-inforcing of errors go undetected, a lifetime of spelling difficulty is likely to ensue.

Introductory Level

Before work on the Introductory Lists begins, check that sound/symbol relationship of all consonants has been acquired.

The majority of sounds may have been mastered, but there may still be areas of confusion. The consonant 'y' can cause problems from infant school to adult-hood. The muddle is often linked with the letter 'u'. The difficulty needs to be isolated and dealt with — it will not simply go away.

Level 1

Level 1 covers a spelling age of 7-9 years. Before work begins Test Dictations should be given. All children should be given Test Dictation A and those with two, or more errors should begin work with the 'a' family.

Test Dictation B should be given to the rest of the class. Those with two or more errors, should begin work with the 'ck' family.

The remainder of the class should begin with the 'ai' family.

Teaching Method

Family Lists

(a) Write word family symbol (a, or, ai, igh etc) in red on the board.

(b) Show card with family words written in blackboard size.

(c) Cover all words except the first — children read it.

(d) Gradually uncover all words until full list is seen.

(e) Draw attention of children to common sound/symbol in all words.

(f) Children now have *new* note-books and pencils.

(g) Children write words as teacher *dictates* them, making sure all sounds are clearly heard.

(h) Encourage children to quietly say the sounds as they write them — especially those who are known to have consonant difficulties.

During the writing of the word family list children do not see words. They listen, say and write. Children can draw small pictures to illustrate words.

Sentences

(a) Encourage children to write a sentence including as many of the words as possible.
(b) Write sentences in rough.
(c) Read sentences to class/group. Others count how many words they can hear belonging to the new family.
(d) Teacher checks all word family lists.

Homework

(a) Take word list home — **or** arrange a few minutes daily in class.
(b) Children read **aloud** word **list** — looking, saying, hearing.

Teaching Points

During the week, make sure that all teaching points relating to a word family and dictation, are covered.

Basic Words

(a) Show children how to finger trace, saying the whole word — **not** sounding it out.
(b) Give children copies of the word.
(c) Allow them to finger trace, saying word six times.
(d) Turn cards over.
(e) Write word **without** looking.
(f) Turn card back and check.
(g) If correct, hand in card.
(h) If not, keep card and finger trace in spare moments until correct.

Dictation

(a) To be given a week after relevant word family list.
(b) To be written under word family list, **in pencil.**

(c) Read slowly and clearly the first sentence or phrase.

(d) Repeat sections of sentence, giving children, even the slow ones, time to write.

(e) Continue to end of dictation in this way.

(f) Children change books with neighbour.
If children are paired good speller/bad speller the following activity can either act as a proof reading exercise for the good speller, or a reinforcement exercise for the poor speller. Pairing must be handled sensitively by the teacher, otherwise, children should keep their own books.

(g) Teacher slowly reads dictation again. Children under-line wrong words.

(h) Pairs discuss wrong words and refer to correct word family, or basic word. Teacher supervises correction activities.

(i) Books returned to owners. Errors rubbed out and corrections made. Teacher checks all dictations.

(j) Children draw pictures in their books to illustrate the story of the dictation. The illustration is part of the reinforcement of the word family — and the children are producing their own story books.

Teach only one word family a week

Remedial Work

As with all remedial work, the child is more important than the method. It is therefore essential that the child's difficulties and spelling stage should be assessed before work begins.

If the work is to be on a one-to-one basis the fundamental principles of
(a) structured phonic work, and
(b) multisensory teaching
remain. The method can then be adapted to the needs of the child, the time available for one-to-one work and integration with the work of the class teacher.

Suggestions

(a) If the class teacher is using these books, the one-to-one remedial teacher could teach the new word family, with the child writing the words from dictation *(no copying)* into a rough note-book, *prior* to the word family being taught in class. He could then create sentences based on the word family and written from the remedial teacher's dictation.

Having covered the ground in a one-to-one situation, he is more likely to benefit from the class lesson. The remedial teacher will begin her next lesson by "testing" the previous week's family. The rule remains — only one new word family should be taught in a week.

(b) If more than one one-to-one remedial session a week is possible and the class teacher is **not** using these books.
  (i)   teach the word family.
  (ii) teach the new basic words with finger tracing method.
  (iii) Cover other teaching points.
  (iv) Give dictation and let the child draw his illustration.

(c) If only one one-to-one remedial session is given a week, the class teacher is not using these books, how the material is adapted depends on the needs of the child. **But** — the essential remains — teach one word family by multi-sensory methods each week. Follow this *either* by the child writing his own sentences
or by the dictation
or by the child reading the relevant instalment, drawing a picture to illustrate it and then making up one or two sentences to describe his picture.

References

Remedial Techniques in Basic School Subjects — Grace M. Fernald.
The Writing Road to Reading — Spalding and Spalding.
Language, Reading & Learning Disabilities — Alexander Bannatyne.

Level 1

Test Dictation A

The dog with the pink drink felt sick. He sat next to the sink. The man held his neck to help him and his soft black hat fell into the sink. The cat jumped up from his bed and ran to sit in the mud.

Two, or more, errors in this dictation indicate that work should begin with the 'a family' and continue at the rate of one new family a week.

Test Dictation B

The free food at the zoo was too much for Tim. He fell asleep in the hot sun. His wife gave his arm a shake. He woke up with a start. They went to the car park and he drove his nice blue car forty miles home.

Two, or more, errors in this dictation indicate that work should begin with 'ee family' and continue at the rate of one new family a week.

The remainder of the class should begin with the 'ai family' and continue at the rate of one new family a week.

Level 1

h a n d
s a n d
s p a t
b a n g
b a n k
c r a m p
t r a p
t r a m p
s p r a n g
s c r a p s

Dictation

The tramp had cramp as he sat with his scraps on the bank. A rat sprang from the sand. The tramp spat at the rat and ran.

Teaching points

(a) Help children to feel '**n**' in hand, sand, bang, bank and sprang. Help them to feel '**m**' in cramp, tramp.

(b) Help children feel 'sp', 'cr', 'tr', 'spr', 'scr' and 'ps'.

(c) Discuss capital letters at beginning of sentences and full stops at the end.

Basic Words

the, he, with, his, on, from.

Level 1

d r o p
s p o t
c o s t
p o n d
f r o s t
l o s t
p l o t
c r o s s
g o n g
s l o t
s t r o n g

Dictation

The cross tramp ran to a spot by the pond. He had lost his scraps, but he had a plot to trap the rat.

Teaching Points

(a) Feel 'n' in pond, gong, strong.

(b) Feel 's' in cost, frost, lost.

(c) Feel 'dr', 'sp', 'fr', 'pl', 'cr', 'sl', 'str'.

(d) Draw attention to 'ss' on cross.

(e) Discuss use of comma.

Basic Words

to, by, but.

Level 1

r i n g
k i n g
s t i n g
m i n t
t r i p
d r i n k
s t r i n g
c r i s p s
p i c n i c

Dictation

The tramp had a string bag. He had crisps in the bag. He sat by the pond and had a drink. The rat ran into the string bag.

Teaching Points

(a) Feel consonant blends, especially 'str' and 'sps'.

(b) Discuss pic/nic.

Basic Words

into.

e

d e s k
t e n t
s e n t
f e l t
h e l d
l e f t
f e l l
s m e l l
y e l l
d r e s s

Dictation

The tramp felt the rat in the bag and held it in his strong hand. He let it smell the crisps. Then, he fell and sent the rat into the pond. He kept the bag in his hand.

Teaching Points

(a) Draw attention to words ending in 'll' and 'ss'.

(b) Feel consonant blends, particularly 'lt', 'ld' and 'ft'.

Basic Words

then.

Level 1

d r u m
d u s t
j u s t
l u m p
b u m p
b u n k
p l u g
s c r u b
h u n d r e d
s u n s e t

Dictation

The tramp had a lump on his leg from the bump. He had no rat in his bag, just dust. The sun set and he held the lump on his leg as he slept. He had no bed and no bunk.

Teaching Points

(a) Draw attention to 'e' in hundred.

(b) Discuss the difference between 'The sunset' and 'The sun set.'

Basic Words

no.

ck

c l o c k
b r i c k
d u c k
l u c k
s n a c k
q u i c k
t r i c k
t r a c k
p e c k
p r i c k
s t r u c k

Dictation

The tramp had bad luck. As he slept, a duck had a peck at his legs and the rat ran back for a quick snack of crisps. The clock struck ten and the tramp sat up.

Teaching Points

(a) As 'ck' together always follow a short vowel, this family can be used to revise short vowel sounds.

(b) Talk about five vowel sounds. Listen hard for which one it is.

(c) Point out that 'u' always follows 'q' in the English language.

ee

s t r e e t

w ee k

q u ee n

s p ee d

s t ee p

b ee

s c r ee n

h ee l

n ee d

s ee d

s w ee p

g r ee d y

Dictation

The Queen is in the street and the fat man needs to sweep the steep track to the pond. The tramp stands up. In his speed, his heel hits a bee. It stings.

Teaching Points

(a) Remind that 'u' follows q.

(b) Discuss capital letters for names — Queen.

(c) Discuss (i) week — meaning days of the week.

(ii) seeds — for the garden.

(iii) heel — of the foot.

(iv) bee — insect

(v) screen — television and cinema.

(d) Discuss 'y' making **ee** sound at the end of greedy.

Level 1

b oo t
b r oo m
r oo f
b e d r oo m
r oo t
z oo m
l oo k
t oo k
w oo d
p oo l
s t oo l

Dictation

The fat man held his broom and had a look at the tramp. The tramp took his boot off to look at his heel. The Queen is on the steep track to the pool and the tramp has no boot on his foot.

Teaching Points

(a) In some areas a change of sound will occur between 'zoom' and 'look'. Discuss this.

(c) Discuss bed/room.

Basic Words
off.

Level 1

c a r
c a r d
y a r d
a r m
f a r m
g a r d e n
h a r d
m a r k
s m a r t
t a r

Dictation

The Queen looks hard at the tramp. He is not smart and his foot is as black as tar. She lifts her arm and the fat man lifts his broom. The tramp just looks at the bee on his boot.

Teaching Points

(a) Draw attention to non-sounding 'e' in 'garden'.

(b) Discuss (i) 'yard' — back-yard, builders' yard, etc.
(ii) 'mark' and 'marks'.
(iii) 'smart' (appearance) and 'smart' (clever).
(iv) tar — the smell, the look, the use.

(c) Discuss the Queen's wave.

Basic Words
she.

or

Level 1

o r
b o r n
t o r n
f o r
f o r t
f o r t y
s t o r y
f o r g e t
m o r n i n g
m o r e

Dictation

The tramp will not forget the morning he met the Queen. The forty TV men will tell the sad story on the screen, but the fat man thinks of the torn boots of the tramp. "We must get more boots and a hot, sweet drink," he says.

Teaching Points
(a) Remind 'y' making 'ee' sound on forty and story.
(b) Draw attention to 'e' on more.
(c) Discuss for/get.
(d) Feel i-n-g on morning.
(e) Show picture of fort.
(f) Discuss for — 'for me', 'for tea', etc.
(g) Speech marks.

Basic Words
TV, says.

sh

Level 1

```
s h e d
s h e e t
s h i p
s h o t
c a s h
c r a s h
r u s h
```

Dictation

The fat man took the tramp to his shed.

"I will rush to get a hot drink for us," he said.

The tramp sat on a sheet of wood and went back to sleep.

Crash! The fat man shot into the shed.

"I forgot my cash," he said.

Teaching Points

(a) Remind about use of speech marks.

(b) Discuss !

Basic Words

said, my.

ch

c h e e k
c h o p
c h i c k e n
c h i p
c h e s t
l u n c h
b e n c h
c r u n c h
s u c h

Dictation

The tramp and the fat man sat on a bench. The tramp had chicken for his lunch and the fat man had a big, pork chop. They had lots of chips.

"I feel good," said the fat man and went to sleep on the bench.

Teaching Points

(a) Draw attention to 'ck' and 'en' in chicken.

(b) Discuss two meanings of cheek.

(c) Feel 'n' in lunch, bench and crunch.

(d) Remind about speech marks.

Basic Words

they.

th

Level 1

t h i n g
c l o t h
m o t h
f r o t h
t h r u s h
t h e
t h e m
t h i s
t h a t
t h e n
t h u d
t h u m p

Dictation

As he slept, a moth struck the fat man's cheek. He fell off the bench with a thud. The tramp sprang to help him. The bench shot up and sent them into the pond. Splash!

They stood up. Green weed clung to them.

Teaching Points

(a) Discuss 's. (man's).

(b) Remind of 'ck' in 'struck'.

(c) Remind !

Level 1

c a m e
g a v e
b r a v e
b l a m e
n a m e
m a k e
s a f e
s a m e
s h a k e
t a k e
t a s t e
w a v e
f a c e

Dictation

The tramp gave a shake and came to the bank. The fat man gave a shake and made such big waves that the ducks swam off. He was stuck in the mud. The tramp came to take his arm. Soon they were safe on the bank.

Teaching Points

(a) Draw attention to soft 'c' in face. 'e' has two jobs — changing ă to ā and making 'c' sound 's'.

(b) Discuss — letters have names as well as sounds. 'e' makes 'a' say its name.

Basic Words

was, were.

Level 1

r i d e
d r i v e
h i d e
m i l e
s m i l e
p i e
t i e
w i p e
i c e
n i c e
s l i c e
s l i d e

Dictation

With a smile, the fat man began to wipe his face with his tie. The wet tramp went to hide in the shed.

"Come on," said the fat man. "Let's ride on the bus to my wife and have a nice, slice of pie."

Teaching Points

(a) Draw attention to 'pie' and 'tie' — no other letter between 'i' and 'e'.

(b) In ice, nice and slice — 'e' has two jobs.

(c) Discuss 's in 'Let's'. (Let us).

Basic Words

began, come, have.

Level 1

```
n o t e
s t o n e
c l o s e
c l o s e d — o p e n
d r o v e
  r o d e
h o m e
h o p e
  r o s e
```

Dictation

The two wet men closed the shed and rode home on the bus. The fat man took his wife one red rose in a stone jar.

"I hope my wife will be at home," he said. "I will give her the rose and hope she will not be cross."

Teaching Points

(a) Draw attention to position of 'e' in 'closed' and 'open'.

(b) Discuss again letter names/sounds.
  Check that all can sequence the alphabet orally.

Basic Words

one, two, her, give.

u—e

b l **u** e
g l **u** e
c l **u** e
t r **u** e
f l **u** t e
t **u** n e
u s e
e x c **u** s e

Dictation

The two men came to the garden gate. The fat man thinks of an excuse to use. It is true that they are very wet, because they sat in the pond.

  "You take her the rose and I'll sing her a sweet tune on my flute," says the tramp.

Teaching Points

(a) Draw attention to blue, glue, clue and true. No other letter between u/e.

(b) Discuss ex/cuse.

(c) Show picture of flute — listen to recording, if possible. Discuss sound.

(d) Discuss I'll (I will).

Basic Words
very, because.

ai

r a i n
p a i n
p a i n t
w a i t
a g a i n
e x p l a i n
a f r a i d
c h a i n
n a i l
s a i l
p a i l

Dictation

The tramp and the fat man are very wet, because they fell in the pond. The fat man looks afraid, as he creeps inside to explain to his wife.

The tramp waits at the gate with his bag and his flute. "I am very wet," says the fat man to his wife, "but not from rain. I sat in the pond again."

His wife has a pail of paint and a paint brush in her hands. A look of pain is on her face.

Teaching Points

(a) Discuss 'again' — in this family, although we usually say 'agen'. Do not write 'agen' — only discuss sound.

(b) Discuss ex/plain, a/fraid. Before dictation discuss in/side.

(c) Discuss 'sail' and 'pail' for meaning, to prevent confusion.

(d) Listen to 'brush' and discuss sounds before dictation.

Basic Words
Revise — says and one.

Level 1

r o a d
s o a p
s o a k
s o a k i n g   w e t
c o a l
g o a l
g o a t
m o a n
o a k
r o a s t
t o a d

Dictation

The tramp stands at the gate with his flute. He is still soaking wet. His hands and face are as black as coal. He has not used soap for many weeks.

He sees that the fat man's wife looks cross. With a soft moan, he grabs his bag and runs back to the road.

Teaching Points

(a) Discuss and feel — 'ing' as in 'ring', 'string', 'soaking'.

(b) Discuss oak tree, with pictures, or actual leaves and acorns.

(c) Discuss, with pictures, the toad.

(d) Discuss 'roast' — as distinct from 'boiled', 'grilled', fried, etc.

(e) Discuss 's — man's wife.

(f) Discuss 'used' (use/used), before dictation.

Basic Words

are, many.

ir

Level 1

g i r l
f i r t r e e
s t i r
s i r
d i r t y
t h i r t y
t h i r s t y
c i r c u s

Dictation

The tramp felt dirty and thirsty. He stood by a fir tree for a rest. A girl rode up to him on a bike.

"Excuse me sir," she said, "are you the tramp with the flute? Please come home for a nice, slice of pie."

The dirty, thirsty tramp took his bag and his flute, then went back with the girl.

Teaching Points

(a) Draw attention to 'y' sounding 'ee', in dirty, thirty and thirsty.
(b) Discuss cir/cus. 'c' sounds 's' when followed by 'i' and 'k' when followed by 'u'.
(c) Discuss 'rode', in silent e family, before dictation.
(d) Discuss ?
(e) Discuss fir trees — Christmas, coniferous, etc.

Basic Words
me, please.

Level 1

house
mouth
sound
round
shout
shouted
aloud
about
count
ground
pound
outside

Dictation

In about thirty seconds, the girl and the tramp stood outside the house. They went round the back. The fat man and his wife were waiting for them.

"My name is Sue and he is Sam," said the wife. "What is your name?"

The tramp opened his mouth and no sound came out.

Teaching Points

(a) Draw attention to final 'e' on house.

(b) Discuss 'ed' on shouted.

(c) Before dictation, remind of 'closed', 'open'. Discuss 'opened'.

(d) Discuss Sue — link with blue, glue, etc.

(e) Discuss 'seconds' — passing of time — and the spelling.

(f) Remind of ?

Basic Words

what, your.

Level 1

t ea
t ea c h
p ea c h
ea c h
c r ea m
s c r ea m
f l ea
r ea d
p l ea s e
s p ea k

Dictation

Sue got out four cups and made the tea. She gave them each a slice of peach pie with cream.

Then she gave a cup of tea to the tramp. A flea jumped out of his coat.

She let out a scream and dropped the hot tea on the tramp's foot.

Teaching Points

(a) Draw attention to final 'e' on please.

(b) Before dictation discuss 's — tramp's foot.

(c) Discuss 'pp' in dropped. Rule is — double the consonant to keep the vowel short.

(d) Remind of 'ed' ending — jumped and dropped.

Basic Words

four.

ay

d a y
t o d a y
T u e s d a y
W e d n e s d a y
m a y
s t a y
a w a y
h a y
t r a y
s t r a y
r a i l w a y

Dictation

The tramp gave a shout. The flea hopped on the tray and the stray cat jumped on the flea.

The stray cat missed the flea and landed on the peach pie.

Sam looked at the mess and groaned.

"It's not my day today."

"Go away and stay away," screamed Sue.

Teaching Points

(a) Suggest children think of 'blue, Tuesday'.

(b) Discuss Wed/nes/day.

(c) Discuss a/way.

(d) Remind of 'ed' ending and doubling consonant to keep vowel short — 'hopped'.

(e) Teach 'it's' (it is). Remind of I'll (I will).

Basic Words

go.

33

ing

(Take off 'e' and add 'ing')

t a k e — t a k i n g
m a k e — m a k i n g
s l i d e — s l i d i n g
s h i n e — s h i n i n g
s m o k e — s m o k i n g
j o k e — j o k i n g
h o p e — h o p i n g

Dictation

Tripping over the stray cat and sliding on the peach pie, Fat Sam went outside. The tramp grabbed his flute and his bag and ran out too. He had been hoping that Sue was joking.

Sam stood by the gate smoking. Taking the tramp's arm, he said "Let's go and sleep in my shed."

Teaching Points

(a) Discuss the rule — take off 'e' before adding 'ing'. Point out that these words are in 'silent e' family.

(b) Remind of doubling consonant to keep short vowel — grabbed, then 'pp' in tripping.

(c) Listen to long vowels (letters saying their own names). Listen to short vowels and link to key words.

(d) Discuss 'Let's' (Let us). Remind of it's and I'll.

Basic Words

too, over.

Level 1

c h u r c h
b u r n t
c u r l
f u r
p u r r
p u r s e
n u r s e
t u r n i p
S a t u r d a y
T h u r s d a y

Dictation

Sam and the tramp went by the church yard. On the ground they found a big turnip and began to eat it.

"It is not as nice as peach pie," they moaned.

"Was that stray cat sent away?" asked the tramp.

"No. She likes that cat with its purr and its fur," said sad Sam.

Teaching Points

(a) Draw attention to 'rr' or 'purr'.
(b) Draw attention to final 'e' on purse and nurse.
(c) Remind ?
(d) Discuss 'its' — "its purr", "its fur" — they belong to the cat.

Basic Words
asked. Revise began.

Level 1

aw f u l
s **aw**
l **aw**
j **aw**
d **aw** n
p **aw**
s t r **aw**
y **aw** n
c r **aw** l

Dictation

Inside the shed by the pond, Sam and the tramp lay on some straw. The tramp gave a yawn and fell asleep. Sam felt awful and was awake until dawn. Then he slept.

As they both slept, the straw began to burn. The smoke woke the tramp and he shook Sam.

"Wake up. Let's get out."

The began to crawl out as the shed burnt to the ground.

Teaching Points

(a) Draw attention to one 'l' at the end of 'awful'.

(b) Discuss the dawn.

(c) Remind — let's (let us).

Basic Words

some, until, both.

oi

o i l
s p o i l
s o i l
n o i s y
t o i l e t
c h o i c e
v o i c e

Dictation

Sam filled a pail from the pond and wet the soil around the burnt shed. He was very noisy as he splashed in and out of the pond.

A voice said, "It is against the law to burn park sheds and spoil the ponds. I have no choice. Come with me."

Teaching Points

(a) Draw attention to: 'e' in toilet; 'y' making ee sound on noisy; to final 'e' on 'choice' and 'voice' making 'c' soft. (A 'c' followed by an 'e', 'i' or 'y' usually sounds 's'.)

(b) Discuss the person behind "the voice".

(c) Listen to 'filled' and 'splashed' — discuss ending.

(d) Discuss 'against' — reminding of 'ai' family and listening to 'st'.

Level 1

r i v **er**
t h u n d **er**
n u m b **er**
n e v **er**
e v **er**
u n d **er**
o v **er**
d r i v **er**
p a r t n **er**
s w **er** v e
k **er** b

Dictation

The policeman took Sam and the tramp to the driver of the police car. They sat in the back and never spoke.

As the driver took the road over the river, it began to thunder and rain ever so hard.

The police car began to swerve. Then, with a crash, it hit the kerb. The police driver fell over.

The tramp jumped out of the crashed car, but his fat partner was stuck.

Teaching Points

(a) Draw attention to final 'e' on 'swerve'.

(b) Discuss 'kerb' and relate it to kerb-drill, if desired.

(c) Discuss partners — choosing partners — doing things in pairs.

(d) Discuss storms — black clouds — thunder — lightning — heavy rain.

(e) Speculate on what the tramp will do — *after* the dictation.

Basic Words

police, (policeman, police car).

Level 1

a l l
f a l l
h a l l
t a l l
w a l l
s m a l l

take off one 'l' to add 'k' or an ending.

t a l k
w a l k
c h a l k
a l w a y s
t a l k i n g
w a l k i n g

Dictation

The tramp wanted to run away. He was too small to help the stuck fat man and the tall policeman was hurt. But he began talking.

"Sit still Sam. I will help the policeman first."

He took the walkie-talkie from the seat and began to call in a small, thin voice.

"Calling all cars. Calling all cars. We have crashed in Riverside Road. Over."

Teaching Points

(a) Discuss — take off one 'l' when adding 'k' or an ending ('always').

(b) Discuss the walkie-talkie and point out 'ie' ending.

(c) Ask which family 'hurt' is in. Then which family 'first' is in.

(d) Break down River/side. Discuss capitals for names of roads.

(e) Make sure all children can write their own address. If not, use finger tracing method.

Basic Words

want, wanted, too (reminder).

Level 1

h ea d
h ea v y
r ea d y
r ea d
i n s t ea d
s w ea t
s p r ea d
b r ea t h
m ea n t
d r ea d f u l

Dictation

The tramp took the policeman's head. It was heavy and he began to sweat. Then hundreds of police cars with flashing blue lamps and noisy hooters came rushing up. They spread out around the crashed car.

Sam and the tramp looked dreadful. The tramp took a deep breath.

"Sorry. Sorry," he shouted. "I only meant one."

Teaching Points

(a) Remind 'y' making 'ee' sound on heavy and ready.
(b) Break down in/stead. Feel 'spr' (spread).
(c) Point out single 'l' on 'dreadful'.
(d) Discuss times when people take a deep breath.

Basic Words

only, sorry. Revise — one, they, hundred.

Level 1

t o w n
c r o w d
f r o w n
f r o w n e d
d r o w n
d r o w n e d
r o w
h o w
h o w e v e r
b r o w
e y e b r o w

Dictation

Policemen began to crowd round the car. They saw the dirty tramp with the hurt policeman and frowned.

They saw how Sam was stuck in the back. The frowns turned to smiles and they began to laugh. Hundreds of policemen stood and laughed. The row drowned the noise of the hooters.

The hurt policeman opened his eyes and sat up. His eyebrows shot up.

"However did all the policemen in town get here?" he asked.

Teaching Points

(a) Discuss 'ed' endings.

(b) Break down how/ever.

(c) Teach 'eye', before 'eyebrow'.

(d) Discuss which family 'dirty', 'hurt' and 'round' belong to *before* dictation.

Basic Words

laugh, laughed, eye, eyes, here.

igh

Level 1

l igh t
n igh t
t o n igh t
m i d n igh t
r igh t
b r igh t
f r igh t
f r igh t e n
f r igh t e n e d
f igh t
h igh
s igh
s igh t
m igh t

Dictation

Sam and the tramp felt frightened. The sight of all those policemen standing in the bright moonlight, made them feel ill.

In a high, thin voice the tramp said, "I called them on your walkie talkie."

The church clock struck midnight and the tramp jumped with fright. He jumped out of the car and ran and ran. He ran away from the laughing policemen and out of sight of Sam who was still stuck in the car.

Teaching Points

(a) Discuss the building of 'fright' to 'frightened', also of 'night' to 'tonight' and midnight.

(b) Discuss the meanings of right. (i) left/right — through activities check that no children have left/right confusion. (ii) right/wrong.

(c) Before dictation *listen* to 'feel ill'. Discuss the sounds and how they are written. Link 'still' with 'ill'.

Basic Words

who. Revise — your.

a (ar)

class
classroom
grass
glass
pass
ask
asked
after
last
blast
fast
path
father
rather
can't

Dictation

Policemen jumped into their cars to chase the tramp. They flashed their blue lights and gave a blast on their hooters. But he was too fast and ran down the path to the long grass. Two policemen ran after him.

"Why didn't you run away?" a policeman asked Sam.

"I can't," groaned Sam. "I'm rather stuck and I can't run fast anyway."

Teaching Points

(a) Discuss regional differences in the sound of this family.

(b) Discuss abbreviations used in colloquial English. Can't (cannot), I'll (I will), I'm (I am), didn't (did not), it's (it is).

(c) Discuss 'too' ('too fast') — revision.

(d) Remind — ?

Basic Words

why, their, any (link with 'many') anyway. Revise — two.

Level 1

(a)
mother
brother
son
other
oven
won
Monday
front
London
month

(b)
come
some
done
glove
love
money
monkey
none

Dictation

Some other policemen came to help Sam. Some tugged from the front and some from the back. At last they won and Sam was out of the car.

"That's my brother," said a short, fat policeman. "Sam you old monkey, what have you done?"

Sam began to explain and the other policemen got quietly into their cars and drove off into the dark night.

Teaching Points

(a) List (a) is largely revision of words learned in Introductory List. Revise this one day and introduce List (b) the next day.

(b) Discuss 'y' saying 'ee' on 'money' and 'monkey'.

(c) Remind of capital letters for days of the week and places.

(d) Discuss meaning of 'won'.

(e) Discuss 'that's' (that is).

(f) Discuss 'monkey' as a term of endearment.

(g) Remind that 'explain' is in the 'rain family'.

(h) Remind — 2 consonants needed to keep vowel short — 'tugged'.

Basic Words

quietly

y (i)

c r y
f l y
f r y
t r y
d r y
s p y
m y
s k y
s h y
w h y

— c r y i n g
— f l y i n g
— f r y i n g
— t r y i n g
— d r y i n g
— s p y i n g
— m y s e l f

Dictation

As Sam was trying to explain, the tramp crept back along the path from the long grass. He had been spying, but was too shy to ask why the other policemen had gone.

"Come home with me," said brother Bob. "My wife is away, so I shall be frying fish for myself."

The two fat brothers walked off. The shy tramp hid again in the long grass. He was by himself and felt like crying.

Teaching Points

(a) Remind of the words learned in Introductory List and show the 'ing' added.

(b) Link 'why' with other question words, already covered in basic words — 'who', 'what' — plus 'when'.

(c) Remind that 'again' is in the 'rain' family.

(d) *After* dictation ask for comments on "Come home." (Look the same — sound different — different families).

Basic Words

gone. Revise — two.

Level 1

s n **o w**
g r **o w**
l **o w**
s l **o w**
b l **o w**
s h **o w**
m **o w**
r **o w**
t h r **o w**

w i n d **o w**
y e l l **o w**
p i l l **o w**
f o l l **o w**
a r r **o w**
m a r r **o w**
t o m o r r **o w**
e l b **o w**
b e l **o w**

Dictation

The tramp began to follow the path back to the pond. He hurt his elbow on a yellow twig which was growing low. He felt very unhappy tonight. Tomorrow things might be better.

Then there was a shout from below. The tramp looked beyond the row of trees. It was the policeman with the big voice.

"Follow me," he said.

Teaching Points

(a) Remind of 'ow' words learned in Introductory List. Move on to new ones — and 'ow' ending.

(b) Point out double consonants to keep vowels short.

(c) Point out single 'l' in be/low. Then introduce be/gan and be/yond, which will be met in dictation.

(d) Discuss double consonants/short vowels to be met in dictation — 'unhappy', 'better'.

Basic Words

Which. Revise — very.

Level 1

                n e w
                f e w
        c h e w — c h e w i n g g u m
                g r e w
                b l e w
                d r e w
                f l e w
            s c r e w
            t h r e w
            k n e w

Dictation

In a few seconds the tramp stood with the policeman. The wind blew and the sky grew dark. The policeman threw the tramp some chewing gum.

"Chew that," he said.

The tramp followed the policeman along the path. The stones hurt his feet and he knew he must get some new boots, but he had no money.

It began to rain hard. The tramp was wet. The policeman looked at him.

"I think you need a hot bath and a few new things," he said.

Teaching Points

(a) Discuss new things — books, toys, clothes etc.

(b) Discuss 'flew' (the bird flew away) and 'threw' (he threw the ball across the room).

(c) Discuss 'knew' — silent 'k' in know and knew. "I know today is Tuesday," "I knew yesterday was Monday," "I know Katy is away today, I knew she wasn't well yesterday."

(d) Discuss ending on 'followed' and divide a/long.

(e) Remind of 'money' family and 'y' ending.

tion

a c **tion**
s t a **tion**
r e l a **tion** — r e l a t i o n s
c o n v e r s a **tion**
i n v i t a **tion**
d e c o r a **tion** — d e c o r a t i o n s
d i r e c **tion**
c o r r e c **tion** — c o r r e c t i o n s

Dictation

The tramp felt frightened as he followed the policeman into the police station.

The policeman had a conversation with some other men and then said, "Now we are ready for action".

He gave the tramp directions to the bathroom. "Take this soap. Have a nice, hot bath and I will visit my relations and get you some new things."

Teaching Points

(a) Discuss 'tion' as the *usual* ending when 'shun' is heard.

(b) If appropriate discuss Action Man.

(c) Discuss relations — brothers, sisters, aunts, uncles etc.

(d) Give them five minutes to have a conversation with a child of their choice — then report on it.

(e) Discuss invitations — birthday, wedding etc.

(f) Discuss Christmas decorations, etc.

(g) Draw attention to double 'rr' in correction/corrections and discuss meaning.

oy

b o y
t o y
j o y
e n j o y — e n j o y e d
a n n o y — a n n o y e d

Dictation

The tramp enjoyed his bath. He remembered when he was a boy and played with his toys in the bath. Now as he grew cleaner, the bath became blacker and blacker. "The policemen will be annoyed, if the bath is so dirty," he said to himself. He got out of the bath to look for a cloth, but there was none.

As he walked round the bathroom, he left pools of water everywhere. He looked at the pools and he looked at the dirty bath. He was frightened and wished he was a boy again, playing with his toys in the bath.

Teaching Points

(a) Point out 'nn' in 'annoy' and 'ed' on 'annoyed' and 'enjoyed'.
(b) Link remembered with 'er' family and get children to feel syllables — re/mem/ber/ed.
(c) Link 'er' ending also to 'cleaner' and 'blacker'.
(d) Remind of o = u family — 'none'.

Basic Words

there, everywhere, water.

59

Level 1

s a u c e
s a u c e p a n
s a u c e r
A u g u s t
a u t u m n
h a u n t e d
f a u l t
a u t o m a t i c

Looks the same — sounds different — sausage — sausages.

Dictation

There was a loud shout from outside.

"Have you had a nice bath?"

"Yes thank you, but I've made rather a mess," said the tramp.

A brown bag was dropped into the bathroom and splashed into a pool.

"Don't worry. Get dressed, then come and have sausages and beans with tomato sauce. There is some hot milk in the saucepan, if you can drink from a saucer. We've just smashed all the cups."

Teaching Points

(a) Remind 'e' making 'c' sound 's' on 'sauce' etc.

(b) Remind of capital letter for months.

(c) Point out 'n' on autumn.

(d) Discuss ways of saying 'fault' (folt).

(e) Divide au/to/mat/ic and discuss automatic things.

(f) Introduce 'sausage' as part of this family, even though it sounds different.

(g) Discuss abbreviations — I've (I have) Don't (do not) We've (we have).

(h) Link 'worry' to 'mother' family and tomato to 'path' family.

Level 1

f i n d
k i n d
m i n d
p i n t
t i d y
t i n y
b l i n d
b e h i n d
l i o n
c h i l d
F r i d a y

Dictation

The tramp looked in the brown bag to see the things the kind policeman had given him. He did not mind what kind of new shirt or trousers he had, as long as they were clean and tidy.

He looked in the tiny mirror behind the shower, but could only see the top of his head.

He went out to the policemen. They smiled to see the tramp in a blue shirt, green trousers and new, brown boots.

He blushed and said in his high, thin voice, "I could not find a cloth to tidy the bathroom. I'm afraid I've left an awful mess behind me."

Teaching Points

(a) Look at the two families in trousers. Add word to both word family lists.

(b) Repeat with shower and also add to 'sh' list.

(c) Talk about 'rr' in mirror.

(d) Feel sounds in bl-u-sh-ed. Talk about blushing and why.

Basic Words

give, given, could. Revise — only.

Level 1

h e a r
e a r
d e a r
n e a r
n e a r l y
f e a r
b e a r d
t e a r s
y e a r

Dictation

The tramp sat down near the kind policeman to eat his sausages and beans with tomato sauce. They gave him a saucer of hot milk from the saucepan. He could not drink it. His long beard flopped into the saucer.

"Oh dear," he said and tears came into his eyes. His beard had not been cut for years.

The kind policeman came near to him with some scissors.

"Have no fears," he said. "We'd better cut that beard."

Teaching Points

(a) Remind that 'sausages' is in the 'au' family like sauce and saucer. Make children think about 'tomato'.

(b) Listen to 'flopped'. Ask how many 'p's' and why. How many 't's' in better?

(c) Abbreviation — we'd (we had).

(d) Look at three tricky bits in sc-i-ss-or-s. Then finger trace as for basic words.

(e) Talk about 'oh' as in 'oh dear', 'oh really', 'oh well' etc.

Basic Words

oh, scissors. Revise — could, eyes.

air

h a i r
h a i r y
f a i r
p a i r
r e p a i r
a i r
c h a i r
s t a i r s
u p s t a i r s
d o w n s t a i r s
f a i r y

Dictation

The policeman took the tramp upstairs to a room with a big mirror. The tramp sat on a chair and the policeman began to cut the beard with a pair of scissors. He cut until the beard was short and smart.

"I think you should cut my hair too," said the tramp.

The policeman cut the tramp's fair hair short round the ears. Then he cut the hair at the back and across the forehead.

"Now come downstairs and show yourself," said the policeman.

The tramp got up from the chair and the pair went back down the stairs.

Teaching Points

(a) Discuss fairs. Also fair (colour) and "It's not fair".

(b) Link 'pair' with — "repair a pair of shoes".

(c) Discuss 'forehead' — pronunciation (fo/red) and spelling 'fore' (meaning front) and 'head'. Link with fore-legs and fore/aft (boats).

(d) Remind of 'too' (as well).

Basic Words

should (link with could).

ou (u)

t o u c h
t o u c h e d
y o u n g
y o u n g e r
c o u n t r y
t r o u b l e
d o u b l e
c o u p l e

Dictation

The couple went back into the downstairs room. The policemen were still eating sausages and beans. They looked up and said to the tramp,

"You look much younger."

The tramp touched his smart hair and beard with his hands and smiled.

"This kind policeman took a lot of trouble. He is a good barber."

Teaching Points

(a) Link 'couple' to 'pair' with regard to people and 'couple' to 'few' with regard to minutes.

(b) Help children to listen to the endings on 'touched' and 'younger'.

(c) Listen to 'barber'. Discuss two families 'ar' and 'er' and add to both lists.

(d) Draw attention to 'le' ending. Most common way of making that sound at the end of English words.

(e) Discuss countries. Have globe, or large map of the world and put marker in countries children have visited — or where they have relations.

Basic Words

Revise — were.

a (o)

s w a n
w a n t
w a s
w a s h
w a s p
w h a t
s w a l l o w
s w a l l o w e d
s w a p
s q u a s h
s q u a b b l e

Dictation

The tramp and the policeman sat down and began to swallow sausages and beans. A bottle of squash was on the table with a glass.

"What would you like to drink? Do you want squash, or hot milk?"

"Squash, please," said the tramp.

As the policeman gave him the glass, a wasp fell into the squash.

The tramp did not see it and took a big gulp. "Stop," said the policeman. "You've swallowed a wasp."

Teaching Points

(a) Link 'what' with 'wh question family' — who, what, why, when, which.

(b) Point out 'll' in swallow and 'bb' in squabble.

(c) Remind of 'le' ending and link with squabble, bottle and table.

(d) Remind of abbreviation 'we've' (we have).

Basic Words

Revise — could and should. Introduce — would.

ph

p h o n e
t e l e p h o n e
p h o t o — p h o t o g r a p h
e l e p h a n t
Ph i l i p
Ph i l i p p a
m i c r o p h o n e

Dictation

The tramp felt the wasp and the squash disappear down his throat. One policeman rushed to the telephone to phone the hospital.

"This is the police station. P.C. Philip Brown speaking. One of our friends has swallowed a wasp. Can we bring him in to you?"

When the tramp heard the policeman on the phone call him their friend, he began to feel very proud.

P.C. Philip Brown left the telephone and came to the tramp with a microphone in his hand.

"Open your mouth wide," he said. "Let's hear if the wasp is still buzzing."

Teaching Points

(a) Discuss other things that begin with tele — television, telegram — and that phone is short for telephone.

(b) Discuss that photo is short for photograph.

(c) Discuss uses of microphones and display one — or a picture.

(d) Link dis/ap/pear with 'ear' family and add to list.

(e) Link throat with 'oa' family and add to list.

(f) Break down hos/pit/al. Draw attention to 'al' ending.

(g) Remind of capital letters for names and discuss that P.C. is short for police constable.

Basic Words

heard (draw attention to 'ear'), friend (point out silent 'i').

o (o)

b o t h
p o s t — p o s t m a n
n o
s o
s o l d
t o l d
 o l d
g o l d
m o s t
 o n l y

Dictation

P.C. Brown put the old microphone into the tramp's mouth. He told the others to be quiet so that he could hear.

At first both the tramp and the policeman heard a faint buzzing. Then it stopped and the only sounds were the tramp's breathing and swallowing.

P.C. Brown went back to the telephone and told the hospital that no buzzing could be heard.

"I think the wasp drowned in squash," he said.

Teaching Points

(a) Remind of apostrophe s — tramp's mouth.

(b) Link faint with ai family and add to list.

(c) Remind of doubling consonant to keep short vowel — stopped and buzzing.

(d) Make sure all children can use a telephone directory.

Basic Words

quiet, put. Revise — could.

c a r e
s p a r e
f a r e
s t a r e — s t a r i n g (s t a r ̸ i n g)
s h a r e — s h a r i n g (s h a r ̸ i n g)
h a r e
d a r e
p a r e n t s

Dictation

The tramp and P.C. Brown sat down again to share the spare sausages and beans. The tramp did not really care about the wasp inside him. He was happy to be sharing a meal with the policemen.

As they sat eating, Sam and his brother came into the police station.

Sam said, "I'm sorry to trouble you, but have you seen my friend the tramp?"

The policemen stared at the tramp, but he did not dare to look up.

Teaching Points

(a) Discuss 'fare' — bus fares etc.

(b) Have picture of a hare and discuss differences with a rabbit.

(c) Point out rule — taking off 'e' to add ing.

(d) Remind of 'trouble' family and of 'again'.

(e) Discuss why the tramp felt shy about looking at Sam.

Basic Words

real, really, sorry (revise).

Level 1

b o u gh t
t h o u gh t
b r o u gh t
o u gh t

Look the same — sound different

r o u g h   c o u g h
e n o u g h
t o u g h

Dictation

"I thought I ought to ask about my friend," said Sam. "He looked rather rough with long hair and a beard."

The policemen began to laugh and P.C. Brown said to Sam, "You haven't looked hard enough."

Sam stared at the tramp in his new blue shirt and green trousers.

Then the tramp thought he ought to speak. "This kind policeman brought me here."

"You old monkey," said Sam and he slapped the tramp hard on the back. The tramp gave a cough and the wasp flew out of his mouth.

Teaching Points

(a) Discuss the group of letters 'ough' and the three different sounds presented here.

(b) Put "bought" and "brought" into sentences when introducing them, to avoid the common confusion.

(c) Abbreviation — haven't (have not).

(d) Remind — 'pp' needed to keep short 'a' in slapped.

ar (or)

Level 1

w a r
w a r n — w a r n i n g
w a r m
r e w a r d
w a r d
q u a r t e r

Teaching Points

(a) Teach only the new family.

(b) Give the children several opportunities to revise word families, in pairs, small groups or at home.
   (i) one child (or parent) reads aloud a "Sam and the Tramp" story, selected at random. Others listen and try to identify relevant word family.
  (ii) if unsuccessful, reader slowly reads words from family until correct response is given.
 (iii) another reader selects the next story, or parent continues.

(c) The following dictations are revision dictations and should be given on two separate occasions as the final pages in the "Sam and the Tramp" story book.

Revision Dictation 1

At a quarter to two, Sue rushed into the police station. She had a warm coat over her nightdress. She was crying.

"I want to offer a reward to anyone who can find my husband," she said as she sobbed. "I've phoned the hospital. My Fat Sam is not in the wards there."

Suddenly, she saw Sam standing near her. She stopped crying and gave him a warm hug.

"Come home," she said. "I will reward you with a nice slice of peach pie."

Revision Dictation 2

Sue turned to the young man standing beside Sam, in the blue shirt and green trousers. She saw his new brown boots, his smart beard and short hair.

"Would you like to come home with us and share the peach pie and cream?" she asked him.

She did not know it was the tramp and Sam did not explain. He thought she might change her mind if she found out and that would be dreadful.

"We would both enjoy that," said Sam. "This is my old friend Augustus."

"Thank you," said Augustus in a quiet voice. "I would love to come. Today is my birthday and I feel like a new man."

"You are a new man," said Sam. "Happy birthday, Augustus. Have a glass of squash."

"Happy birthday," sang all the others.

After revision dictations all books should be collected and a record kept of each child's difficulties with

(i) word families

(ii) basic words

(iii) sequencing of letters and syllables within words.

Further work should be planned in areas of difficulty.